Senses

Tasting
in Living Things

Karen Hartley, Chris Macro and Philip Taylor

Heinemann
LIBRARY

First published in Great Britain by Heinemann Library,
Halley Court, Jordan Hill, Oxford OX2 8EJ
a division of Reed Educational and Professional Publishing Ltd.
Heinemann is a registered trademark of Reed Educational & Professional Publishing Ltd.

OXFORD MELBOURNE AUCKLAND
JOHANNESBURG BLANTYRE GABORONE
IBADAN PORTSMOUTH (NH) USA CHICAGO

Designed by Celia Floyd
Illustrated by Alan Fraser
Originated by Ambassador Litho Ltd, UK
Printed in Hong Kong / China

05 04 03 02 01
10 9 8 7 6 5 4 3 2 1

ISBN 0 431 09731 3
This title is also available in a hardback library edition (ISBN 0 431 09724 0).

British Library Cataloguing in Publication Data

Hartley, Karen
  Tasting in living things. – (Senses)
  1. Taste – Juvenile literature
  2. Sense organs – Juvenile literature
  I. Title II. Macro, Chris III. Taylor, Philip
  573.8'78

Acknowledgements

The Publishers would like to thank the following for permission to reproduce photographs:

Bruce Coleman: Jane Burton p.22, MPL Fogden p.17; Corbis: Kennard Ward p.16; FLPA: Winifred Wisniewski p.23; Heinemann: Gareth Boden p.4, p.5, p.6, p.7, p.8, p.11, p.13, p.15, p.24, p.25, p.26, p.27, p.28, p.29, Trevor Clifford p.10; Image Bank: P Goetgheluck p.20; Oxford Scientific Films: Steve Turner p.18, Tom Ulrich p.21; Pictor International p.14; Tony Stone: Peter Cade p.19, Roy Gumpel p.9.

Cover photograph reproduced with permission of Oxford Scientific Films and Gareth Boden.
Many thanks to the teachers and pupils of Abbotsweld Primary School, Harlow.

Every effort has been made to contact copyright holders of any material reproduced in this book. Any omissions will be rectified in subsequent printings if notice is given to the Publisher.

For more information about Heinemann Library books, or to order, please telephone +44 (0)1865 888066, or send a fax to +44 (0)1865 314091. You can visit our web site at www.heinemann.co.uk

Any words appearing in the text in bold, **like this**, are explained in the Glossary.

Contents

What are your senses?

People and animals have senses to help them find out about the world. You use your senses to feel, see, hear, taste and smell. Your senses can warn you of danger.

Your senses are very important to you and other animals every day. This book is about your sense of taste. You are going to find out how it works and what you use it for.

What do you use to taste?

Some people think we can taste things with our teeth but our teeth only bite and chew. You use your front teeth to bite your food. You chew food with your **molars**.

You taste things with your tongue. The tongue can only taste things when it is wet. **Saliva** keeps your mouth wet. The **roof** of your mouth can taste things too.

How do you taste things?

You can only taste something if it is in your mouth or touching your tongue. There are tiny lumps on the edges of your tongue and in your mouth called **tastebuds**.

In the picture you can see tastebuds on a tongue. When they taste something they send a message to your brain. Your brain can remember lots of different tastes.

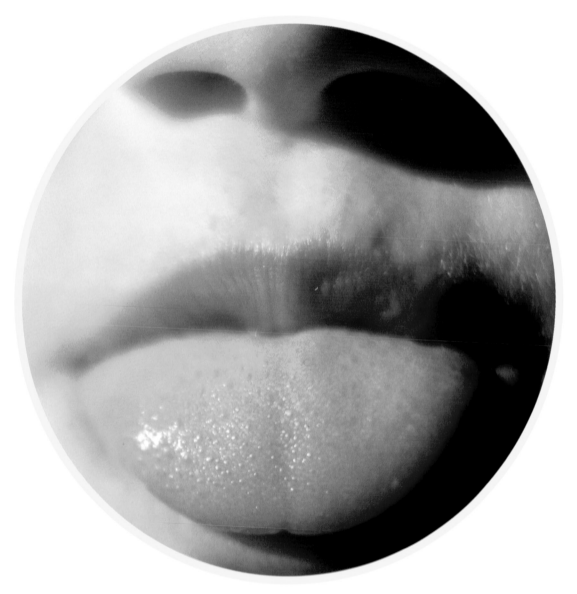

How taste helps you

When you taste something your brain knows what you have put in your mouth. You eat food because you like the taste. You have to eat food so that you stay **healthy**.

Often if you taste something which is not safe to eat, your brain tells you to spit it out quickly. Sometimes your brain cannot tell if it is bad for you, so you must not eat or drink something you do not **recognise**.

How do you use taste?

The **tastebuds** on different parts of the tongue can taste when foods are salty like potato crisps, sweet like chocolate, sour like a lemon or bitter like the olives on a pizza.

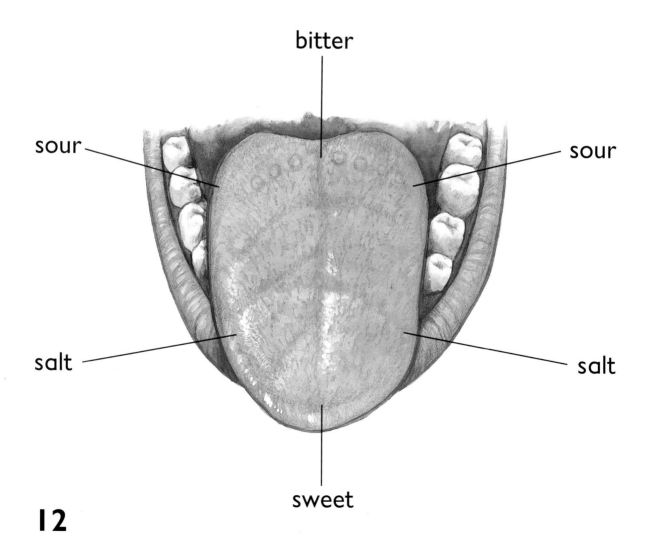

bitter

sour

sour

salt

salt

sweet

When you put something into your mouth, your tongue **recognises** if it is hard or soft, hot or cold. It can also recognise if it is big and round like the sweet in the picture.

Why do things taste funny?

Your brain needs smell and taste messages to **recognise** food properly. When you have a bad cold you cannot always smell things very well so then your food tastes funny.

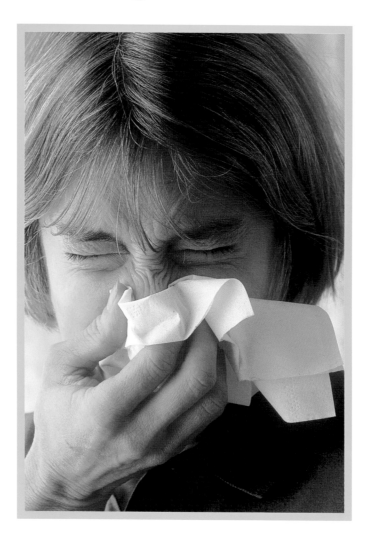

Very hot things can burn the **tastebuds** and then they cannot taste things properly for a little while. This also happens if you suck an ice lolly and make your tongue very cold.

How animals use taste

Some animals have **tastebuds** that work like yours. Chimpanzees like some of the food that you eat because they taste things the same way you do.

Some animals like things that taste even sweeter than sugar. A humming bird likes to eat **nectar** from flowers. **Insects** like butterflies like the taste of nectar.

More about animals

Many animals like the taste of different plants. Giraffes like the new tender leaves that grow on the trees in summer. These are very good for the giraffes.

Can you think of any animals that eat grass? A sheep's tongue can taste lots of different **flavours** in a **clump** of grass.

Unusual ways to taste

Most animals have **receptors** that taste their food. Sometimes they are very different to our tongues. A spider has special **feelers** called **pedipalps** to taste things.

Lizards and snakes have a receptor in the **roof** of the mouth to smell and taste things. A snake waves its tongue and pushes the air onto the receptor so it can taste it.

Using taste to keep safe

Most animals like cats and dogs smell their food before they taste it. If it smells bad they do not eat it. If they taste something they do not like they spit it out.

Most birds do not have any **tastebuds**. Ostriches eat anything that will fit in their mouth and go down their throat! Parrots do have tastebuds so they can taste their food.

Investigating taste

If you look very carefully at someone's tongue you can see little bumps on it. These are the **tastebuds** that taste your food. Can you remember how they work?

In the picture you can see things which are sour, salty, sweet and bitter. If you tasted each of these things which part of the tongue would recognise the **flavour**?

Playing tricks on taste

Your sense of taste sends a message to the brain more slowly than your other senses. If you smell an onion whilst you are eating an apple you might think you are eating an onion!

If food looks different you can think it tastes different. Your eyes send a message to the brain more quickly than your **tastebuds** do. Would you like the taste of green potato?

Did you know?

An adult has about 3000 **tastebuds** and a child has even more! The tastebuds begin to die as you grow older. Old people do not taste their food as well as children do.

When you think about eating something your mouth begins to make **saliva**. This helps you to taste things. In your **lifetime** you will make enough saliva to fill a swimming pool!

Glossary

clump a tuft of grass or plants

feelers thin growths from the head of an animal that help the animal tell what is around it

flavour the way something tastes

healthy not ill

insects small animals with six legs

lifetime as long as people live

molars the big teeth at the sides and back of your mouth

nectar a sweet sugary juice inside flowers

nerve something that carries messages from the body to the brain

receptors tiny parts in the body which can sense what is around it

recognise to know what something is

roof the top of the mouth

pedipalps special feelers which spiders use to taste food

saliva the spit which is made in the mouth to keep it wet

tastebuds lots of taste receptors in a group

Sense map

brain recognises the taste messages

tongue **recognises** the shape of the food

taste **receptors** on the tongue (**tastebuds**)

saliva comes from under the tongue to make food wet enough to swallow

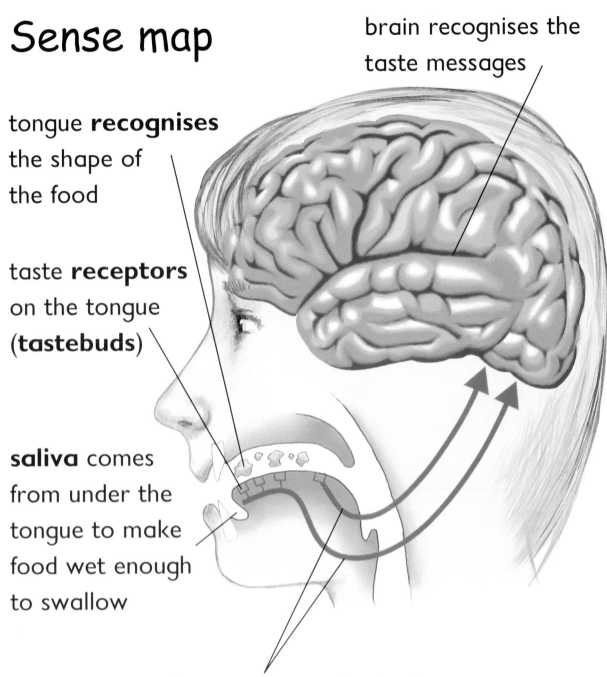

nerves carry the message to the brain

Index